The Mind Reboot Toolkit:

TRANSFORM YOUR THOUGHTS TO CHANGE YOUR LIFE

Rachel Boyer, LMHC

VOLUME 1

Insightful Solutions Therapy, LLC

Copyright

ISBN: 9798993945408
Printed in the United States of America
First Edition, Volume 1

You can download free resources and printable versions of the trackers in this workbook by visiting www.InsightfulSolutionsTherapy.org or using the QR Code below, and accessing the "Resources" section.

Your Reboot Begins

This workbook is here to help you learn how to understand your thoughts, manage emotions, and take action that supports real change.

The Chapters are ordered in a way that will help you build a foundation, but you can start where it makes sense. Use what's helpful. Come back to what you need. Complete this on your own, or with guided support. The journey is yours.

This book belongs to:

_____

_____

_____

_____

Wishing you the best on your
self-improvement journey!

~Rachel Boyer, LMHC
Insightful Solutions Therapy

Introduction- Goal Setting

First step........goals.

In therapy, we talk a lot about change. But change only becomes possible when we clarify what needs our attention and identify the shifts we'd like to see. It's important to know where you are starting from, and where you want to go.

Here, you will walk through your own patterns and identify your core concerns. You'll then map out your goals in a structured way so that you can revisit them over time to see if you are on track. You can add to or adjust your goals at any point.

Rachel Boyer, LMHC
INSIGHTFUL SOLUTIONS THERAPY

Identifying Your Core Issues
What am I Really Struggling With?

This worksheet will help you to walk through your patterns of thoughts, feelings and behaviors, and identify your core concerns. Being honest here helps you build a more accurate and compassionate picture of what you're facing—and what you're capable of shifting.

First: Identify your core concerns
Start with broad themes like anxiety, self-esteem, motivation, sadness, shame, or difficulty asserting yourself. These are starting points—not definitions.

Then: Describe what the issue looks like in your life
How does this show up in your thoughts? How do you feel emotionally? What kinds of behaviors follow?

General issue:
One or two words that capture the core concern.

What it looks like:
In your everyday life. It shows up when....

Thoughts:
That typically pop up in these moments.

Emotions:
Your usual feelings that accompany this issue.

Behaviors:
How you respond (or don't respond) when this happens?

Goal Setting

Clarifying What You Want to Change

Before any meaningful change happens, it's important to know where you are starting from, and where you want to go. Change becomes possible when we clarify what needs our attention and identify the shifts we'd like to see. Work on setting personal and specific goals that feel reachable.

Steps to Goal Setting

Step 1: Define your primary challenge This is a broad description of what you would like to improve.	
Step 2: Identify specific goals to address that challenge What would you like to change ? What would you want life to feel like? How do you want to act or think?	
Step 3: Name actions that support those goals This helps you track progress. Think of actions as small indicators that you're moving toward change—even if the feelings haven't caught up yet.	

Examples

Challenge: Low self-esteem.
Specific Goals: I want to feel more confident expressing myself and speaking in groups without feeling invisible.
Supporting Actions: Making a list of strengths weekly, initiating one conversation per day, and asking for feedback at work.

Step 1: Define your primary challenge

Step 2: Identify specific goals to address that challenge

Step 3: Name actions that support those goals

Rachel Boyer, LMHC
INSIGHTFUL SOLUTIONS THERAPY

Investing in Change
Why?

Recognizing the benefits of change can motivate you, especially during tough times. Keep your "why" in mind to understand the purpose behind the change. Consider a goal you'd like to work on and identify the pros (benefits) and cons (drawbacks) of making that change. What might you gain or lose? What challenges might you encounter along the way?

My Goal: _____

PROS

CONS

VS

What might get in the way of your attempts to change?

What are some ways to address these barriers?

Reboot Reflection

This page is yours to explore any thoughts, themes, or insights that stood out. You'll also find a few guiding questions to support your reflection.

One personal goal I'm ready to work on:

One small action I can take:

One insight or pattern I noticed...

Something I want to remember...

Rachel Boyer, LMHC
INSIGHTFUL SOLUTIONS THERAPY

Cognitive Behavioral Therapy

Cognitive Behavioral Therapy (CBT) is widely known as one of the most effective methods for addressing stress-related challenges. This therapy emphasizes the connections between our thoughts, emotions, and behaviors.

Through CBT, you will discover how to recognize, alter, and reframe negative or unproductive thinking patterns. Ultimately, these adjustments will foster healthier thought patterns and lead to changes that positively influence your moods and behaviors.

On the following pages, you will find an introduction to the fundamentals of CBT, along with worksheets to help you apply CBT techniques to reshape your thoughts and improve your life.

Rachel Boyer, LMHC
INSIGHTFUL SOLUTIONS THERAPY

How Change Takes Place
Using CBT

Learn Skills

You learn skills that will help you first identify thoughts, beliefs, and assumptions that influence your responses in specific situations. These thoughts tend to be automatic and are not always noticed.

Identify Thoughts

Example: "Dogs Bite!"

"Dogs Bite! This dog will bite me."

Examine Facts

Once you identify the thoughts, you can examine the facts, both good and bad, for and against, your automatic thoughts. We call these facts "evidence."

- Dogs do bite
- I was bitten last year
- Not all dogs bite
- Only 1% of people are bitten
- I have met friendly dogs

Adjust the Original Thought

Following examination, use the facts you discover to re-adjust your original thought. Looking at this evidence provides a new outlook on the situation. This is called "restructuring" or "reframing."

"Some dogs bite, but only a small percent and usually when they are afraid."

Make Informed Choices

With this new outlook, you are able to make more informed choices on how to respond to the situation.

"This dog does not seem threatening. I am o.k. with standing near it."

Have Better Outcomes

Changing your thoughts and how you respond to the situation can lead to improving how you feel in life.

"I feel less anxious around this dog and can go on without running away."

The CBT Model
Thoughts, Emotions and Behaviors

CBT is based on the idea that our thoughts, emotions, and behaviors are closely connected. When one of them shifts, the others often respond—sometimes in helpful ways, sometimes in ways that keep us stuck. Understanding this connection is the first step toward change.

Thoughts

We interpret situations all day long—whether through words, memories, or mental images. Some thoughts are helpful and accurate. Others are automatic, shaped by past experiences, and may be distorted or overly negative. These thoughts can strongly influence how we feel, even if we aren't fully aware of them.

Feelings

Emotions are often responses to thoughts:
"I always mess up" → feeling ashamed
"They must be mad at me" → feeling anxious
"I don't matter" → feeling hopeless

These emotions can cause physiological symptoms like a racing heart or sweating. Understanding the thoughts behind these emotions allows for thoughtful questioning and responses.

Behaviors

How we act is often shaped by how we feel. Feeling anxious might lead us to avoid a situation. Feeling hopeless might make it harder to follow through with self-care or plans.

Sometimes our behaviors help relieve distress in the short term—but they might reinforce the same negative thought, keeping the cycle going in the future.

Rachel Boyer, LMHC
INSIGHTFUL SOLUTIONS THERAPY

The CBT Model

Thoughts, Emotions and Behaviors

According to CBT, our thoughts, in response to a situation or "trigger," influence our feelings and behaviors. Our feelings and behaviors can then influence our thoughts, and also influence one another.

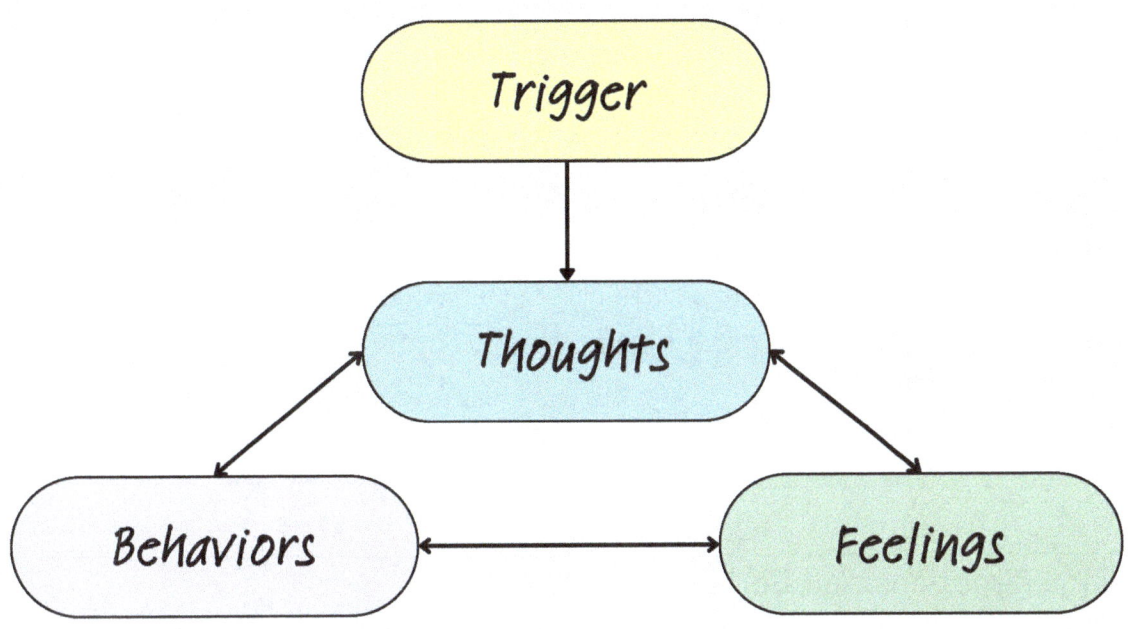

Example: "I Did Something Wrong!"

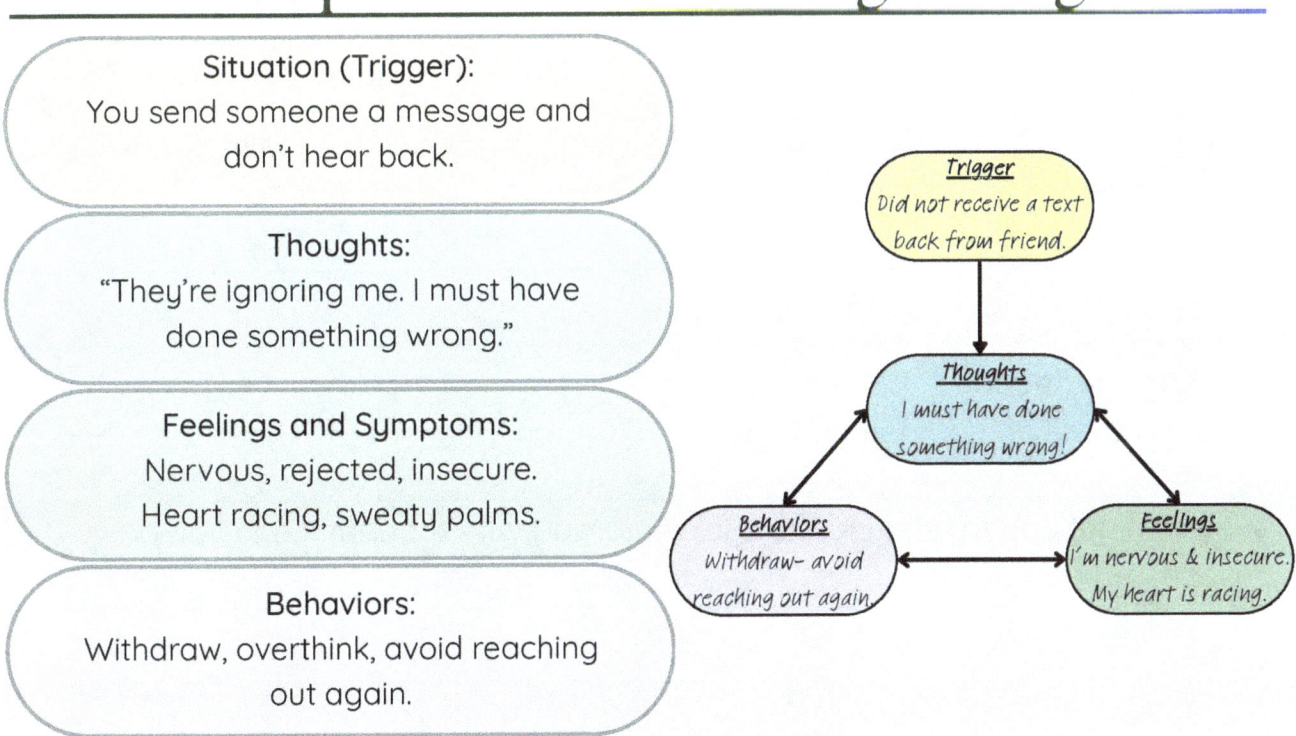

Situation (Trigger):
You send someone a message and don't hear back.

Thoughts:
"They're ignoring me. I must have done something wrong."

Feelings and Symptoms:
Nervous, rejected, insecure. Heart racing, sweaty palms.

Behaviors:
Withdraw, overthink, avoid reaching out again.

Thoughts, Feelings & Behaviors

Directions

Think of a moment from this past week when you felt overwhelmed, anxious, sad, frustrated, or emotionally activated. Use this page to identify the details of that experience. You don't need perfect answers—just be curious as you reflect.

Situation

What happened? Describe the situation briefly.

_____

_____

Thoughts

What ran through your mind? These might be words, mental images, or assumptions. (Examples: "I can't handle this," "They think I'm incompetent," "This will never get better")

_____

_____

Feelings (Emotions and Body Sensations)

What emotions came up? What did you notice in your body? (Examples: anxiety, sadness, heaviness, racing heart, tight chest, tears, flushed face)

_____

_____

Behaviors

What did you do—or avoid doing? What was your response? (Examples: withdrew from conversation, procrastinated, canceled plans, criticized self)

_____

_____

Optional Reflection

What patterns do you notice? Does one component seem to trigger the others?

_____

Where might you try shifting the cycle—starting with thought, behavior, or response?

_____

_____

Rachel Boyer, LMHC
INSIGHTFUL SOLUTIONS THERAPY

Mood Tracking

How to Track Emotions

Our emotions don't always show up with clear labels. Sometimes we feel a swirl of feelings. Other times, we feel numb and disconnected. The goal is to begin gently observing your mood—without judgment or over analysis—so you can develop a clearer picture of how emotions are shaping your thoughts and behaviors.

Steps to Mood Tracking

Step 1: Write down a short, factual description of the situation

Step 2: List the emotions you felt

Step 3: Rate the peak intensity of each emotion (scale of 1–10)

Step 4: Describe any sensations in your body

Examples

"Argued with friend,"
"Was alone all evening," "Thought about an upcoming deadline"

Use one-word: anxious, sad, embarrassed, angry, hopeless, nervous, excited, proud

1 = mild
5 = moderate
10 = overwhelming

Racing heart, tight chest, nausea, heaviness, sweating, dizziness, fatigue

Example: Car Panic Attack

Date & Time	Situation (Just the facts)	Emotions (1 word each)	Intensity (1-10)	Body Sensations
8/25 4pm	My sister was driving the car fast.	Anxious Scared Angry	8	Heart racing, palms sweaty, breathing heavy

Monitoring Moods

Directions

Use this worksheet to track your emotional experiences over the next seven days. You can fill it out once per day or complete it throughout the day as you notice mood shifts. Notice how your emotional states unfold in real time.

Date & Time	Situation (Just the facts)	Emotions (1 word each)	Intensity (1-10)	Body Sensations

Rachel Boyer, LMHC
INSIGHTFUL SOLUTIONS THERAPY

Automatic Thoughts

What?

We all have automatic thoughts. Sometimes they pop up unexpectedly, other times we may not even notice them. Unhelpful negative automatic thoughts about ourselves, others, or the world around us are called "hot thoughts."

Why?

Automatic thoughts are shaped by our prior experiences. Sometimes, these thoughts are to protect ourselves. Our brain wants us to survive and warns us of potential danger. Sometimes, the danger is overestimated, and our thoughts can cause us more damage than good.

Type of Unhelpful Thoughts

Overestimating danger or thinking negative outcomes will happen.

Catastrophizing. The outcome will be awful and there will be no way to cope.

The anxiety itself is dangerous, and will cause craziness or a loss of control.

The outcome, discomfort, or pain will be intolerable.

Excessive worry is thought to be helpful to prepare for possible outcomes.

Negative assumptions about the self, others, or the world.

Which ones resonate with you? _____

Identifying Automatic Thoughts

What?

Automatic thoughts are involuntary and are based on our core beliefs about ourselves, others, and the world around us. Sometimes they are difficult to identify because it can be uneasy to confront them. It's not uncommon to have a hard time noticing these thoughts or knowing your underlining core beliefs.

Why?

Identifying negative automatic thoughts is the first step in the process of "restructuring" them to lead to better outcomes. This is a skill that needs to be practiced consistently. When we continuously practice this skill, we are literally training our brain. Our brain will begin to recognize these thoughts, and it will become more natural.

How?

To identify and prepare for restructuring your thoughts, it is necessary to create a thought record. You can track your thoughts a number of ways:

- Daily, as situations arise
- Recalling past events
- Imagining a scenario
- Role playing a situation

When you document your thoughts, you will need to do two things to prepare for restructuring:

1. Phrase the thought as a statement

"What if the dog bites me?" **-->** "The dog will bite me"

2. Be specific

"I'm afraid something will happen" **-->** "I'm afraid I'll be bitten and get infected"

Use the upcoming thought tracker in this workbook to begin tracking your automatic negative thoughts.

Rachel Boyer, LMHC
INSIGHTFUL SOLUTIONS THERAPY

Identifying "HOT" Thoughts

How to Do it

Unconscious thoughts often arise automatically and can shape our emotions and behaviors. "HOT" thoughts, which are negative and unhelpful, may affect how we feel, and spotting them can be tricky. The following questions can assist in identifying these automatic thoughts.

What just ran through my mind?
(This is often clearest when the emotion is strong)

What does this situation mean to me?
(Look for the interpretation you've assigned)

What's the worst part of this — and why?
(Your fear or pain might uncover the thought)

What emotion did I feel—what thought could explain it?
(Work backward from emotion to thought)

Thought Tracker
Directions

Use this worksheet to track your thoughts over the next seven days. You can fill it out once per day or complete it throughout the day as you notice mood shifts. Notice how your emotional states unfold in real time.

Date & Time	Situation (Just the facts)	Emotions and Body Sensations	Intensity (1-10)	Thoughts

Rachel Boyer, LMHC
INSIGHTFUL SOLUTIONS THERAPY

Cognitive Distortions

What?

Our emotions can influence our thinking. Sometimes, we have patterns of thinking that are extreme, focused on negatives, and not based on facts. There are different types of common cognitive distortions that people experience.

Why?

Once we identify cognitive distortions in our thought patterns, we can start adjusting them.

Distortion	Description
Black-and-White or All-or-Nothing Thinking	We see things as either all good, or all bad. There is no in-between "grey zone."
Catastrophizing	We respond as if something is the worst thing ever.
Jumping to Conclusions, Mind Reading, or Fortune Telling	We predict something bad will happen without any evidence to prove this.
"Shoulds"	We criticize ourselves or others with what "should" be done and ignore the reasons why it may have been done (or not been done) that way.
Ignoring the Positive or Filtering	We focus on negatives of a situation, and ignore or reject the positives.
Overgeneralization	We see an isolated event as a constant pattern of defeat. The following terms are common: always, everything, never, nothing.
Blaming	We believe others are responsible for how we feel.
Emotional Reasoning	We believe the way we feel reflects realty or the truth of a situation.

Which ones resonate with you? _____

Thought & Distortions Record

Directions

Track any stressful thoughts (HOT thoughts) that come up, the situation that sparked those thoughts, your feelings (emotions and bodily sensations) and any cognitive distortions you may notice. Use direct statements (rather than "What if?") and be specific. This will help bring attention to your thoughts, and prepare you for the skill of restructuring. Sometimes a thought will fall under more than one cognitive distortion. Try this over the next week.

Note: Sometimes thoughts lead to other thoughts. Capture these as well.

Situation	HOT Thoughts	Feelings	Cognitive Distortions

Rachel Boyer, LMHC
INSIGHTFUL SOLUTIONS THERAPY

Cognitive Restructuring

What?

Cognitive restructuring is a process of examining evidence both for and against our thoughts, which helps us to make a realistic assessment of a situation, and form a more rational response.

Why?

Our thoughts can filter our perceptions. When we examine facts, it helps us to see things more clearly and allows us to adjust how we see a situation. This may impact how we react and how we feel.

Example: "He Hates Me!!"

I said hello yesterday to this person I am trying to be friends with. He walked right by me without saying hi back, and he didn't even look at me!

HE HATES ME!

Evidence For	Evidence Against
He did not look at me	He said hi to me yesterday
He did not say hi to me	He has never said anything rude to me
He has not called me his friend	He asked to sit next to me on Monday

Our perceptions do not always reflect reality. In the example above, the individual who failed to say hello might have been preoccupied and simply did not hear the greeting. This understanding would evoke a different response and emotion compared to the thought, "He must hate me."

Alternative Thought: HE DIDN'T RESPOND. HE MAY HAVE NOT HEARD ME. I'LL TRY AGAIN NEXT TIME.

Try the Tracker on the next page to begin identifying evidence both for and against stressful thoughts.

Cognitive Restructuring

Track any negative thoughts that come up, the situation that sparked those thoughts, and evidence for and against those thoughts. When considering evidence, think about the likelihood of the thought being true, facts that support and rebut the thought, and the actual impact that the thought may have if it was true.

Situation	HOT Thoughts	Evidence For	Evidence Against

Rachel Boyer, LMHC
INSIGHTFUL SOLUTIONS THERAPY

Cognitive Restructuring
How?

In order to restructure our thoughts, we need to examine the evidence and get closer to the truth of the situation. There are two types of questions that help us analyze our thoughts after identifying the facts.

Question #1:

How likely is it that your thought is true?

- **What is the percent likelihood of this thought?**
  - How sure am I?
- **What evidence do I have that supports that this thought may be valid?**
  - What evidence shows that it may not be?
- **How many times have I predicted this before?**
  - How many time has it happened when I predicted it?

We tend to overestimate. Asking this will help us realistically assess the situation.

Question #2:

If it did happen, how bad would it be?

- **Would I be able to cope?**
- **What would I do?**
- **Would I eventually get over it?**
  - Will it matter in a day, a week, a month, a year?

We tend to catastrophize. Asking this will help us see if we can cope with a negative outcome.

Cognitive Restructuring

Continue your weekly tracking. This time, monitor any negative thoughts that arise, along with the situations that triggered them, and gather evidence both supporting and contradicting those thoughts. Next, analyze this evidence by applying the thought-challenging questions from the previous page. This approach will assist you in restructuring or reframing the original thought in a way that promotes a more positive mindset.

Situation	HOT Thoughts	Evidence For or Against	Response to Challenge Questions

Rachel Boyer, LMHC
INSIGHTFUL SOLUTIONS THERAPY

Cognitive Restructuring
The Final Step

To reduce stress, restructure your thoughts using cognitive skills. Identify HOT thoughts, examine evidence, recognize distortions, and apply problem-solving and acceptance skills. Use the below form to practice evaluating a thought and reframe or restructure the thought for a more balanced perspective on your situation. You can measure how effective this is by rating the intensity of emotions both before and after you complete this process.

Step #1: Identify the negative automatic thought:

Step #2: List the cognitive distortion(s):

Step #3: Explore the evidence:

Question 1: Likelihood	**Question 2: Severity**
How likely is this thought?	If the thought did happen, could I cope?
How sure am I?	What would I do?
Have I predicted this before?	Would it matter in another day, week, month or
Has it come true before?	year?

Step #4: Write down the evidence:

Step #5: Adjust your thoughts and if needed- problem solve:
Is there another way to view this? Is there a way to improve the situation?
Are there things outside of my control that I can't change and can let go?
What can I do to adjust or cope?

TIP: If your negative thought frequently occurs, write your evidence on something you can carry with you as a reminder. Re-read it when you have the thought.

Reboot Reflection

This page is yours to explore any thoughts, themes, or insights that stood out. You'll also find a few guiding questions to support your reflection.

A common HOT thought I have:

How has it affected my daily life?

What's a recent situation where my thoughts shaped my emotions or actions?

What emotion tends to show up often for me?

One insight or pattern I noticed...

Something I want to remember...

Rachel Boyer, LMHC
INSIGHTFUL SOLUTIONS THERAPY

Core Beliefs

Core beliefs influence how we perceive ourselves, others, and the world around us. By recognizing and transforming negative core beliefs, we can effectively change our thoughts, feelings, and actions.

In this section, you'll start to uncover some of your core beliefs (which can be quite challenging!) and contemplate the origins of these beliefs you've acquired.

Rachel Boyer, LMHC
INSIGHTFUL SOLUTIONS THERAPY

Core Beliefs

What are Core Beliefs?

Core beliefs are deep thoughts or assumptions we have about ourselves, other people, and the world. They act like invisible filters that shape how we see and experience life. There are both helpful and unhelpful core beliefs.

Examples of *Unhelpful* Core Beliefs

"I'm not good enough"
"I'm worthless"
"I'm bad"

Self

"People can't be trusted"
"Everyone is judging me"
"Nobody cares"

Others

"The world is a bad place... is dangerous... things happen for a reason"

The World

Where Do They Come From?

Family and upbringing
School and friends
Social media and culture
Life experiences—especially strong memories

Why They Matter

They influence how we think, feel, and act
They shape how we handle problems, relationships, and challenges
They can create "auto-pilot" thoughts that feel true... **even if they're not**

Can Beliefs Change.............YES!!

Beliefs can shift through reflection, honesty, and practice.

Ways to start:
　　Notice patterns like "I always..." or "I never..."
　　Ask yourself: Is this always true? Where did I learn this?
　　Test out new beliefs with small actions

Unhelpful Core Beliefs - Examples

Self

I'm not good enough
I'm broken
I'm unlovable
I always mess things up
I'm worthless
I'm invisible
I'm a burden to others
I'm weak
I'm not smart enough
I'm too sensitive
I don't deserve happiness
I can't handle stress
I'm not interesting
I'm a failure
I need to be perfect
My feelings don't matter
I'm always the problem
I'm incapable of change
I'm too damaged to be helped
I don't belong anywhere
I ruin everything
I can't trust myself
I'm a disappointment
I'm too emotional
I'm not creative
I'm unworthy of love
I'm only valuable when I'm productive
I'm not attractive enough
I'm too slow
I'm not enough
I don't deserve rest
I'm not allowed to say no
I'm not strong enough
I can't cope without others
I'm defined by my past mistakes

Others

People will leave me
Others can't be trusted
People only like me when I'm useful
No one really listens to me
Others are judging me constantly
People are out to hurt me
Relationships always end badly
I'm always being used
If I'm honest, people will reject me
Others will think I'm weak
People just pretend to care
I have to earn love
If I ask for help, I'm needy
People don't understand me
I must never upset anyone
Everyone else is doing better than me
Others only care about themselves
People always disappoint me
I'm never really safe with others
If I'm vulnerable, I'll be hurt
Others always see my flaws
I have to please everyone
No one can be trusted
People are better without me
Others will betray me
I'm always being judged
People will exploit me
If I let people in, I'll lose control
I always have to prove myself
People only like the version of me I pretend to be

The World

The world is unsafe
Nothing ever goes right
Life is meaningless
Bad things always happen
The world is cruel
You can't count on anything
Everything ends in loss
Good things don't last
There's no room for mistakes
The world doesn't care about me
Success requires sacrifice
You can't trust the future
Life is a constant struggle
There's never enough
People suffer for no reason
Joy is fleeting
You have to earn your worth
Safety is temporary
If something feels good, it must be wrong
The world is always watching
Justice doesn't exist
You must always be on guard
Vulnerability is dangerous
Only the strong survive
Hope is naïve
Everyone is out for themselves
You have to fight for everything
If you slow down, you'll fall behind
The future is bleak
There's no space for someone like me

Rachel Boyer, LMHC
INSIGHTFUL SOLUTIONS THERAPY

Core Beliefs: Downward Arrow

What?

Core beliefs are beliefs about yourself, others, and the world. These beliefs have been learned through your experiences, and guide you to judge what is right and wrong, true and false, good and bad. Sometimes these beliefs are not helpful and lead to or fuel unhelpful thoughts.

THOUGHT: My friend didn't call me. She is so inconsiderate.
WHAT DOES THIS MEAN?

⬇

She isn't really my friend.
WHAT DOES THIS MEAN?

⬇

I don't have friends who care about me.
WHAT DOES THIS MEAN?

⬇

There's something wrong with me if others don't care.
WHAT DOES THIS MEAN?

⬇

I'm not worth caring about.
WHAT DOES THIS MEAN?

⬇

CORE BELIEF: I am worthless.

Why?

Uncovering our beliefs allows us to replace them with healthier and more helpful beliefs.

How?

One technique used to help uncover core beliefs is called the "downward arrow technique."

Using this technique, start by identifying an automatic thought that has been bothering you. Ask yourself, "what does this mean (about me, others or the world), or what if this was true?"

Keep going until you arrive at your core belief.

Core Beliefs: Your Experiences

Directions

To get an idea of where some of your core beliefs may have developed from, reflect on your previous experiences. A few journal prompts are listed below.

Which people have made the biggest impact in your life?

What have you learned from them?

What negative messages did you get about yourself from others?

What did you learn about yourself going through hard times?

What are the earliest memories you have of any of the core beliefs?

How did your caregivers communicate with you that may have shaped your core beliefs?

What reocurring patterns in life have supported these beliefs?

Rachel Boyer, LMHC
INSIGHTFUL SOLUTIONS THERAPY

Core Beliefs: Timeline

Directions

Utilize this template to document the experiences and interactions you've had with individuals or situations, including caregivers, teachers, peers, and cultural influences. These factors may have played a significant role in shaping your core beliefs over time. List the core beliefs you think these experiences have shaped in you.

Events	Ages	Self	Others	The World

Core Beliefs: What are Yours?

Directions

After reflecting on some of your unhelpful automatic thoughts, list out the core beliefs you identified.

I Am...

Core
Beliefs

Others Are...   The World Is...

Rachel Boyer, LMHC
INSIGHTFUL SOLUTIONS THERAPY

Changing Core Beliefs
How?

Changing a core belief is challenging and requires time and practice. To replace a negative belief, create a balanced new one and focus on evidence supporting it. Engage in experiences that reinforce this belief, leading to a gradual decrease in the negative core belief as the positive one takes its place. In the next few pages, you will be provided with examples of healthy core beliefs, and ways you can instill them in your life.

Old negative core belief I would like to adjust:

Rate (0-100%) How much I believe it now: How much I believe it when it's most convincing: How much I believe it when it's least convincing:	**Associated Emotions:**

New balanced core belief I would like to adopt:

Rate (0-100%) How much I believe it now: How much I believe it when it's most convincing: How much I believe it when it's least convincing:	**Associated Emotions:**

Old Negative Core Belief

Evidence for:	**Alternative ways of looking at the evidence:**

New Balanced Core Belief

Evidence for (past and present):	**Evidence for (what to look for in future):**

Things I can do to support or gain more evidence for my New Balanced Core Belief:

Rate how much (0-100%) I believe the old negative core belief now:	**Rate how much (0-100%)** I believe the new balanced core belief now:

Healthy Core Beliefs - Examples

Identity in Relationships

I am allowed to set boundaries.

I can be kind without losing myself.

I am not responsible for others' emotions.

I am allowed to say no.

I can choose who I allow into my life.

I am worthy of reciprocal relationships.

I can be loved for who I truly am.

I am allowed to protect my peace.

I can be connected without being consumed.

I am learning to trust safe people.

I can be vulnerable and still be strong.

I am allowed to leave what harms me.

I can be honest and still be loved.

I am not too much or too little—I am just right.

I can be both independent and supported.

I am allowed to choose myself.

I can be present without performing.

I am learning to honor my needs in relationships.

I can be both soft and powerful.

I am worthy of connection that feels safe.

Existence & Belonging

My existence matters.

I deserve to take up space.

I am allowed to ask for support.

I can be important to someone.

I am worth listening to.

I can make a difference.

I am allowed to rest.

I can be loved without performing.

I am not too much.

I am not a burden.

I can be safe with others.

I am allowed to change.

I can be trusted.

I am worth showing up for.

I can belong.

I am allowed to have needs.

I can be seen and still be safe.

I am worth protecting.

I can be enough, even when I'm struggling.

I am allowed to take care of myself.

Self-Worth & Identity

I am enough, even when I feel uncertain.

I am allowed to take up space.

I am worthy of love and respect.

I am more than my past.

I am a whole person, not a broken one.

I am learning to see myself clearly.

I am allowed to define who I am.

I am valuable, even when I'm not productive.

I am not my mistakes.

I am allowed to grow and evolve.

I am a person in progress, not a finished product.

I am allowed to be proud of myself.

I am worthy of being seen and heard.

I am not responsible for being perfect.

I am allowed to be different.

I am learning to trust my own voice.

I am not a label—I am a layered story.

I am worthy of belonging.

I am allowed to change my mind.

I am not defined by others' opinions.

Rachel Boyer, LMHC
INSIGHTFUL SOLUTIONS THERAPY

Healthy Core Beliefs - Examples

Accountability & Integrity

I can take responsibility without losing my worth.
I can make amends and still be a good person.
I can learn from my actions.
I am capable of growth through honesty.
I can hold myself accountable with compassion.
I am learning to repair what I've hurt.
I can be honest without being harsh.
I am allowed to own my story.
I can choose integrity over perfection.
I am learning to align my actions with my values.

I can be trustworthy and still make mistakes.
I am allowed to reflect and revise.
I can be responsible without carrying blame.
I am learning to respond, not react.
I can be both accountable and kind.
I am allowed to grow from feedback.
I can take action toward repair.
I am learning to lead with intention.
I can be a safe person for others.
I am allowed to evolve my beliefs.

Self-Compassion

I am allowed to forgive myself.
I can be gentle with myself while I grow.
I am learning to soothe my own pain.
I am allowed to rest.
I can hold space for my emotions.
I am not weak for needing support.
I am allowed to feel joy, even in hard times.
I can be kind to myself in moments of struggle.
I am learning to speak to myself with care.
I am allowed to grieve what I've lost.

I can hold both sadness and hope.
I am not alone in my healing.
I am allowed to feel deeply.
I can be patient with my process.
I am learning to accept my imperfections.
I am worthy of compassion.
I can comfort myself without judgment.
I am allowed to ask for help.
I can be my own source of safety.
I am learning to love myself in pieces.

Narrative & Meaning

I am the author of my own story.
I can rewrite the messages I've internalized.
I am allowed to question old beliefs.
I can choose how I interpret my experiences.
I am not the story others told about me.
I am allowed to find new meaning.
I can create a life that reflects who I truly am.
I am learning to honor my truth.
I can find beauty in imperfection.
I am allowed to redefine success.

I can choose what I carry forward.
I am not stuck—I am unfolding.
I can find wisdom in my wounds.
I am allowed to be the narrator, not just the character.
I can shape my future with intention.
I am learning to trust my inner compass.
I can find clarity through reflection.
I am allowed to reframe my past.
I can create meaning from my experiences.
I am not a victim—I am a survivor with agency.

60 Ways to Support a New Core Belief

Use this list to help reinforce a belief you're working on—like "I am worthy," "I can regulate my emotions," or "I have agency." Choose 3–5 to try this week.

Daily Actions

☐ Write the belief in your journal each morning
☐ Say it aloud while brushing your teeth
☐ Set it as your phone wallpaper
☐ Create a sticky note reminder on your mirror
☐ Choose one behavior that reflects the belief and do it today
☐ Track moments when the belief felt true
☐ Pair the belief with a breath cue
☐ Build a playlist that reflects the belief's energy
☐ Choose clothing that makes you feel aligned with the belief
☐ Use the belief as a mantra during transitions

Behavioral Experiments

☐ Ask for help and observe the response
☐ Say no to overcommitment
☐ Try a new skill or recipe
☐ Set a boundary with someone you trust
☐ Make a decision without over-researching
☐ Speak up in a group or session
☐ Choose expressive movement
☐ Reflect on a past success
☐ Practice eye contact or open posture
☐ Share a personal truth with someone safe

Emotional Anchoring

☐ Visualize yourself living from the belief
☐ Use grounding techniques while repeating the belief
☐ Journal about how the belief feels in your body
☐ Pair the belief with a calming scent or texture
☐ Create a "belief breathwork" ritual
☐ Use movement to embody the belief
☐ Reflect on how the belief shifts your reactions
☐ Practice self-compassion when the old belief resurfaces
☐ Create a collage or art piece
☐ Write a letter from your future self

Social & Environmental Reinforcement

☐ Spend time with people who speak to you with warmth
☐ Join a support group or forum aligned with your belief
☐ Attend a workshop or retreat that reinforces the belief
☐ Follow creators who model the belief
☐ Share your belief journey with someone who validates you
☐ Visit emotionally safe and identity-affirming spaces
☐ Volunteer in ways that reflect your values
☐ Practice the belief in low-stakes social settings
☐ Curate your digital environment to support the belief
☐ Reflect on how relationships shift when you act from the belief

Rituals & Reminders

☐ Light a candle while repeating the belief
☐ Sip tea or water slowly while reflecting on it
☐ Create a belief card to carry in your wallet
☐ Stack the belief with an existing habit
☐ Record a voice memo of the belief
☐ Use a visual anchor (stone, bracelet, photo)
☐ Set a calendar reminder with the belief
☐ Create a "belief altar"
☐ Write the belief on a whiteboard or chalkboard
☐ Celebrate small wins—name them out loud

Identity Integration

☐ Speak from the belief, not about it
☐ Use values-based language
☐ Build a weekly schedule that reflects the belief
☐ Choose one relationship to show up differently in
☐ Reframe a setback as evidence of growth
☐ Create a "belief log" with tags like #proof
☐ Practice saying the belief aloud
☐ Role-play how you'd act if the belief were true
☐ Reflect on how the belief changes your self-talk
☐ Write a new narrative that includes the belief

Rachel Boyer, LMHC
INSIGHTFUL SOLUTIONS THERAPY

Living a New Core Belief

How?

Use this worksheet to reflect on your experience as you practice living from a new core belief. You can complete it after trying a few activities from the "60 Ways to Support a New Core Belief" list on the previous page, or use it weekly to track your growth.

1. What is the new core belief I'm working on?

Write the belief in your own words. Make it feel authentic and emotionally grounded.
Example: "I am safe enough to rest." "I am worthy of care." "I can regulate my emotions."

_____

_____

2. What activities did I try to support this belief?

List 3-5 actions, rituals, or experiments you practiced this week.
You can reference the 60-item list or add your own.

_____

_____

3. What felt most supportive or surprising?

Describe what helped the belief feel more real, or what caught you off guard.
Did anything shift emotionally, physically, or relationally?

_____

_____

4. How did my body respond?

Tune into your physical experience. Did you feel more grounded, tense, open, or calm?
You can also note any movement, breath, or sensory cues that helped.

_____

_____

5. What internal voices or old beliefs showed up?

Notice any resistance, doubt, or old narratives that surfaced.
How did you respond to them?

_____

_____

6. What evidence did I gather that this belief is true?

List moments, interactions, or feelings that support the new belief.
These can be small or subtle—every bit counts.

_____

_____

7. What do I want to try next?

Choose 1-2 new activities, behaviors, or environments to explore next week.
You can also revise your belief if it's evolving.

_____

_____

Reboot Reflection

This page is yours to explore any thoughts, themes, or insights that stood out. You'll also find a few guiding questions to support your reflection.

A core belief I have uncovered is...

How has this impacted my life?

One insight or pattern I noticed...

Something I want to remember...

Rachel Boyer, LMHC
INSIGHTFUL SOLUTIONS THERAPY

Values and Sense of Self

Values are the qualities, principles, and ways of living that matter most to you—like honesty, creativity, connection, or growth. Unlike goals, which can be completed, values are ongoing directions that guide how you want to show up in life.

Understanding and clarifying what is meaningful to you is important to developing a strong identity.

Clarifying your values helps you make decisions that feel aligned, even during moments of stress or uncertainty. It also strengthens motivation and emotional resilience by connecting your coping strategies to what truly matters.

Rachel Boyer, LMHC
INSIGHTFUL SOLUTIONS THERAPY

Developing a Sense of Self

Your Unique Identity

Your sense of self is how you perceive yourself- who and what you believe you are. This sense of identity could include your values, personality, and relationships. Accepting yourself for who you are, believing you can change to who you want to become, and practicing authenticity can lead to a stronger sense of self.

Your Values

Understanding and clarifying what is meaningful to you is important to developing a strong identity. You can then align your beliefs with your actions. Knowing who you are and what you stand for gives you a greater sense of purpose. Sometimes, our lives don't align with our values, and lack of self-confidence gets in the way.

Reflection helps to know what values you have, and values you would like to improve upon or develop. **Pick 3-6 values that are important to you. Then, choose one and write about what it means to you on the next page- why it's important, how you express it (or would like to express more of it) in your daily life.** A list of examples is below.

Acceptance	Enthusiasm	Justice	Practicality
Accomplishment	Equality	Kindness	Productivity
Altruism	Ethicality	Knowledge	Reason
Artistic	Excellence	Leadership	Reliability
Nature	Excitement	Learning	Resourcefulness
Awareness	Expressive	Love	Risk
Beauty	Fairness	Loyalty	Security
Bravery	Faith	Mastery	Service
Calm	Family	Maturity	Silence
Carefulness	Freedom	Meaning	Simplicity
Commitment	Friendship	Mindfulness	Skillfulness
Community	Generosity	Nature	Spirituality
Compassion	Gratitude	Openness	Spontaneity
Confidence	Growth	Optimism	Stability
Contentment	Happiness	Originality	Strength
Connection	Harmony	Patience	Thoughtfulness
Creativity	Health	Peace	Understanding
Curiosity	Honesty	Persistence	Uniqueness
Dependability	Humility	Personal	Trustworthiness
Dignity	Humor	Growth	Truth
Discipline	Individuality	Spirit	Welcoming
Empathy	Intuitiveness	Wisdom	
Energy	Joy	Play	

Developing a Sense of Self

Your Values: Reflection

Pick one value and write about what it means to you- why it's important, how you express it (or would like to express more of it) in your daily life.

Rachel Boyer, LMHC
INSIGHTFUL SOLUTIONS THERAPY

Developing a Sense of Self

Your Values: Reflection

Reflecting allows you to understand your current values and identify those you wish to enhance or cultivate.

Take some time to reflect by responding to the questions below.

What is important to you? What do you truly value (not what other people think you should care about)?

What sort of person do you want to be at work? In your relationships? In your community?

If you could wave a magic wand and have your ideal life, what would that look like? How would you feel and act?

Reboot Reflection

This page is yours to explore any thoughts, themes, or insights that stood out. You'll also find a few guiding questions to support your reflection.

What values are important to me?

What can I do to strengthen them?

One insight or pattern I noticed...

Something I want to remember...

Rachel Boyer, LMHC
INSIGHTFUL SOLUTIONS THERAPY

Techniques for Depression

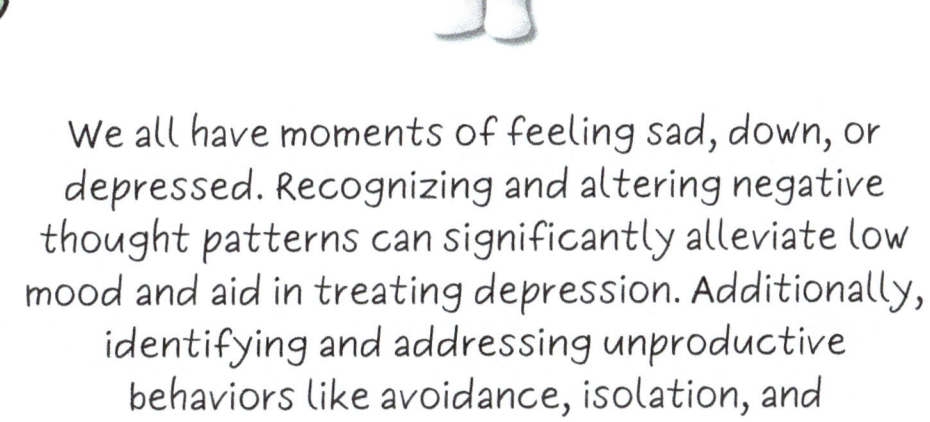

We all have moments of feeling sad, down, or depressed. Recognizing and altering negative thought patterns can significantly alleviate low mood and aid in treating depression. Additionally, identifying and addressing unproductive behaviors like avoidance, isolation, and procrastination will help in feeling relief.

In this section, you will explore the cycle of depression along with various treatment techniques designed to enhance your mood.

Continue to apply the CBT skills you've learned to combat depressive thoughts. These techniques, along with any additional support you may need, such as medication or therapy, will make a substantial difference.

Rachel Boyer, LMHC
INSIGHTFUL SOLUTIONS THERAPY

Behavioral Activation

Why?

The symptoms of low mood or depression can keep us stuck in a negative cycle, and prevent us from feeling better.

For example, when we have low energy, we may avoid activities or tasks. However, doing less activity or not engaging in things we use to enjoy only makes us feel less motivated and tired. Avoiding responsibilities make us feel overwhelmed and guilty.

Depression

Low Energy & Interest

Less Activity & Tasks

Hopelessness & Guilt

Reversing the Cycle

The first step to breaking this cycle is to increase your activity level through "Behavioral Activation." This means scheduling activities (both pleasurable and responsible) even if you don't feel like doing them. This schedule will help you to shift your focus, feel more energized, and feel more in control, ultimately leading to some improvement in mood.

Behavioral Activation for Depression

How?

You can help reverse the depression cycle by increasing your activity level and engaging in pleasurable activities, responsibilities, exercise, healthy routines and self care. Use this weekly activity schedule to plan your week and schedule activities that will help you feel more hopeful, confident, energetic and motivated. Be sure to include a balance of enjoyable activities with your daily responsibilities.

Time	Mon	Tues	Wed	Thurs	Fri	Sat	Sun

Rachel Boyer, LMHC
INSIGHTFUL SOLUTIONS THERAPY

Rumination

What?

We all ruminate sometimes—especially when faced with difficulty. But not all thinking is helpful. Rumination is a learned habit that may have developed from early life experiences. In the past, it may have helped you feel safe or prepared, but now it keeps you stuck. **New habits can replace old ones - with awareness and repetition.**

Helpful Thinking vs. Getting Stuck

Thinking that leads to problem-solving and action is useful.
Thinking that loops, judges, or avoids action creates stagnation.

Rumination vs. Reflection

	Rumination	Reflection
Thought Style	Repetitive, circular	Curious, focused
Focus	"Why did I mess up? What if...?"	"What happened? What can I do next time?"
How You Feel	Anxious, ashamed, stuck	Clearer, compassionate, more balanced
Result	No action or clarity	Insight or small next step

Activity: Rumination vs. Reflection

Use this after a stressful thought spiral or anytime your brain is stuck on repeat, to identify if your thoughts are ruminative or reflective.

- **What triggered the loop?**
- **What thoughts replayed?**
- **Label Them: R for Rumination, or F for Focused Reflection.**

Tip: If it's abstract, blaming, "what-if," or past-focused with no resolution—it's likely rumination.

If the thoughts are rumination, use an "attention switch." Do something different like physical activity, music or grounding.

What will be your attention switch? _____

Interrupting Unhelpful Rumination

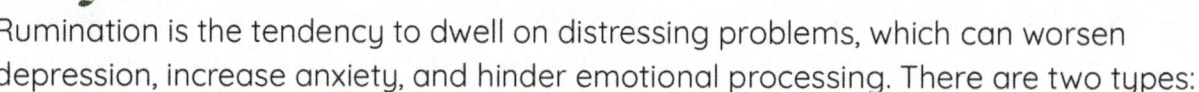

Why?

Rumination is the tendency to dwell on distressing problems, which can worsen depression, increase anxiety, and hinder emotional processing. There are two types:

- **Reflection:** Involves problem-solving questions (e.g., "What can I do to improve this situation?").
- **Unhelpful Rumination:** Focuses on "why" questions that dwell on problems and their causes (e.g., "Why do bad things happen to me?").

How?

Question the accuracy and purpose of your thoughts; challenge them if necessary.

Distract yourself with physical activities, music, or conversation if thoughts are unhelpful.

Create a plan to address problems by writing down realistic goals and timelines.

Identify triggers to effectively manage them.

Cultivate healthy habits, such as self-esteem, self-compassion, self-care, and supportive relationships, to combat negative thinking.

> What are some ways I can solve this problem?
> _____
> _____
> _____
> _____

> How can I make this situation better?
> _____
> _____
> _____
> _____

> Action steps to address the problem
> _____
> _____
> _____
> _____
> _____

56

Interrupting Rumination

How?

Below are a few examples of ways to interrupt rumination. Try one per week, and see if any work for you. Use the tracker below to keep track of what you try, when you try it, and the results.

Schedule Worry Time	• Schedule a worry time. Set a 10 minute timer to worry. • If worries pop up outside of this window, tell yourself you will think about it during your worry time.
Externalize the Worry	• Imagine your worry as a balloon or cloud outside of yourself. • Describe or draw what it looks like (color, size, shape, etc.). • Then, blow it away and watch it float off.
Prepare with Intention	• Create a script: "If I catch myself worrying in the morning, then I will....." • Plan an action such as using a guided breathing video, engaging in physical activity or listening to music.
Self-Compassion Pause	• When you notice self-judgement, place a hand on your heart and whisper a kind phrase (i.e., "May I be gentle with myself"). • Repeat this phrase quietly for 30 seconds.
Pattern-Play Prompt Jar	• **Materials**: Small slips of paper, jar, pens • **Instructions**: Write pattern prompts (e.g. "draw 10 wavy lines," "fill a page with circles," "create a grid of dots")—fold and drop into a jar. When stuck in thoughts, pick one and draw it.

What I tried

When I tried

The Results

Reboot Reflection

This page is yours to explore any thoughts, themes, or insights that stood out. You'll also find a few guiding questions to support your reflection.

What's one thing I want to do that will help my mood?

What is my plan to carry this out?

One insight or pattern I noticed...

Something I want to remember...

Rachel Boyer, LMHC
INSIGHTFUL SOLUTIONS THERAPY

Techniques for Anxiety

Avoidance of things that make us nervous, anxious, or worried, can protect us in the short term—but over time, it shrinks our world. It limits our experiences in life. Exposure techniques help you gently face feared situations with support, pacing, and intention.

In these next few pages, you will learn about what Exposure is, how it works, and identify how to approach anxiety in an actionable way through having an Exposure plan.

Exposure to stressful events is best done with the help of a therapist or trained guide, who can support you along the way.

Rachel Boyer, LMHC
INSIGHTFUL SOLUTIONS THERAPY

Exposure
Why?

Avoiding triggers that cause anxiety prevents people from confronting the trigger they perceive as "dangerous." This only maintains and even heightens anxiety toward that trigger. Gradually exposing ourselves to the trigger, beginning with small steps, allows us to tackle the anxiety directly. By acknowledging and experiencing the anxiety while also challenging unproductive thoughts, we can gradually instruct our amygdala (our brain's "alert" system) to relax.

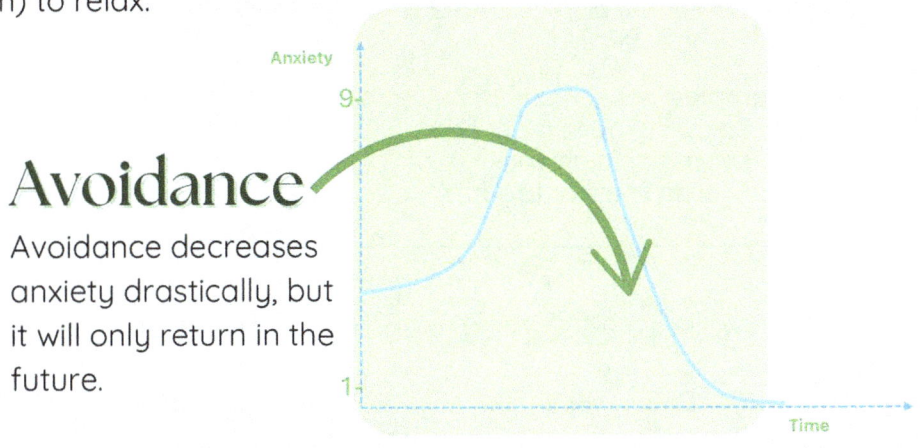

Avoidance

Avoidance decreases anxiety drastically, but it will only return in the future.

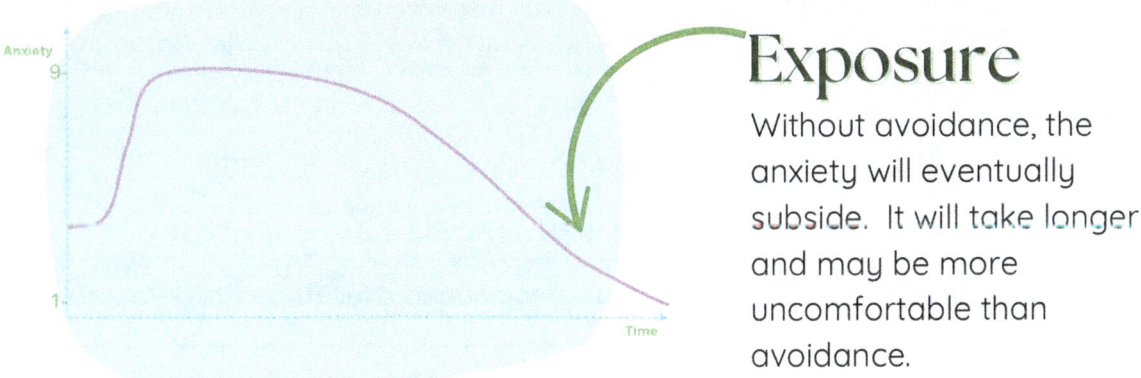

Exposure

Without avoidance, the anxiety will eventually subside. It will take longer and may be more uncomfortable than avoidance.

Repeated Exposure

With repeated exposure, the intensity and duration of the anxiety lessen over time. This is much more effective for long-term recovery.

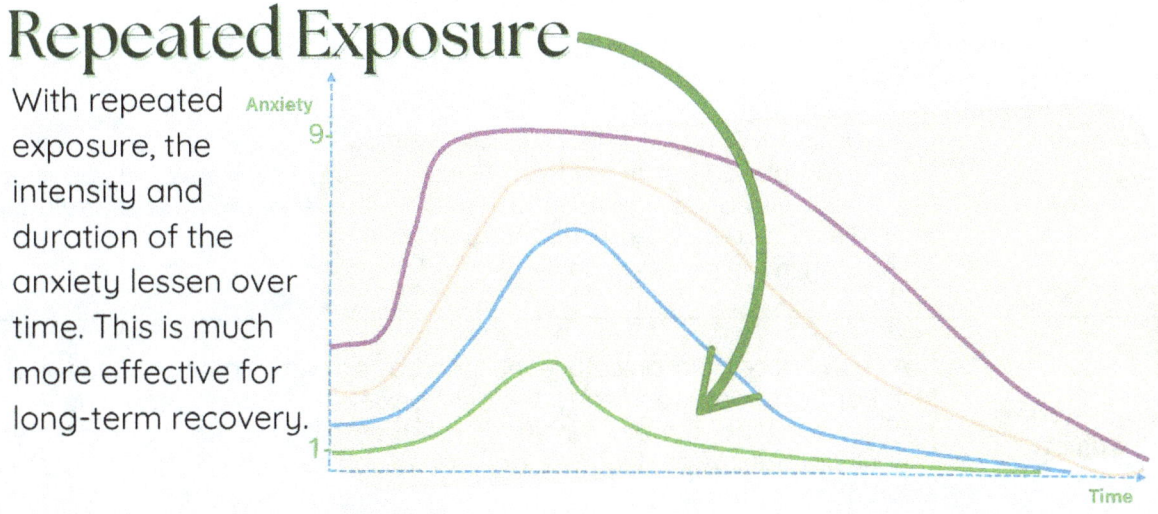

Exposure: Step-by-Step Guide

Why?

Exposure helps retrain your brain to respond more calmly to anxiety triggers. By gradually facing feared situations, thoughts, or sensations, you will build confidence, regulate your physical anxiety response symptoms, and reduce avoidance. The steps are outlined here, and the following pages will help guide you on completing these steps.

Step 1: Identify Your Triggers	List specific situations, thoughts, or sensations that provoke anxiety. Be as concrete as possible. **Examples:** • Speaking up in meetings • Driving on highways • Feeling short of breath
Step 2: Rate Your Level of Anxiety	You will use a 0-100 rating to assign to each trigger.
Step 3: Create Exposure Steps	Choose an anxiety trigger that is in the "mild" anxiety range, and break it down into manageable steps. These are your "Exposure Steps." Start with the least anxiety-provoking situation first. You will move through intensity levels only as you become comfortable with the less anxious situations. **Example:** Anxiety trigger → social gatherings (anxiety rating: 30) Exposure Steps: • Step 1: Text a friend to chat (Rating: 10) • Step 2: Meet one friend for coffee (Rating: 15) • Step 3: Attend a small group hangout for 30 minutes (Rating: 25)
Step 4: Schedule and Repeat	Plan exposures 3-5 times per week. Repetition builds tolerance and confidence. **Tips:** • Continue to repeat each Step in your Exposure Plan until your discomfort has lessened before moving on to the next Step. For example, do not move from Exposure Step 1 to Step 2 until your anxiety has decreased significantly with Step 1 after doing it repeatedly. • Track anxiety before, during, and after exposure. • Stay in the situation until anxiety decreases (don't escape early).
Step 5: Reflect and Adjust	As you notice your anxiety levels decreasing with repetition, you will work toward exposing yourself to the next anxiety-provoking Step. The "Exposure Plan" template includes more details on this process. Ultimately, you will continue to decrease anxiety as you expose yourself to more intense situations.

Rachel Boyer, LMHC
INSIGHTFUL SOLUTIONS THERAPY

Anxiety Rating Scale

Why?

One effective method for addressing anxiety is to confront the things that cause us distress. By literally "facing our fears," we can learn how to handle them. As we engage with the situations that evoke fear, we discover our ability to manage anxiety. Over time, we realize that our fears lessen as we come to understand that what once felt threatening is not truly harmful.

How?

On the next page, jot down as many triggers of anxiety that you can think of. These can include situations, thoughts, or physical sensations, as well as things you tend to avoid. Rate each item on a scale from 0 to 100, using the descriptions provided below. Be sure to include triggers with varying levels of anxiety.

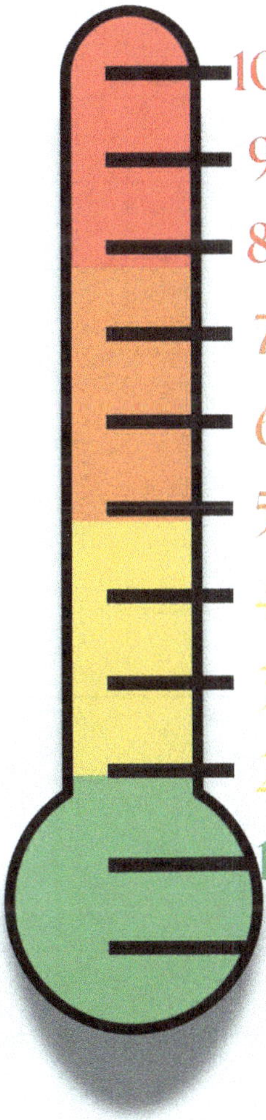

100: Highest distress ever felt

90: Extremely distressed

80: Very distressed. Can't concentrate

70: Quite distressed. Difficulty functioning

60: Strong distress. Physiological signs

50: Moderately uncomfortable but functioning

40: Mild to moderate distress

30: Mild distress. No interference with functioning

20: Minimal distress

10: Alert, awake. Concentrating well

0: No distress. Totally relaxed

Anxiety Rating Scale
How?

Identify triggers that make you anxious. These could be things such as situations, thoughts, physical sensations, or things that you avoid. Anything counts. Rate each item on a scale from 0 to 100 intensity, using the descriptions provided on the previous page. Be sure to include triggers with varying levels of anxiety.

Anxiety Level	Trigger	Rating	Trigger	Rating
Mild				
Moderate				
Severe				

Rachel Boyer, LMHC
INSIGHTFUL SOLUTIONS THERAPY

Exposure Plan

Feel free to use this template to define and track the steps of your exposure plan. Refer to page 62 as needed. There is also a Exposure Tracking Form on the next page.

Anxiety Provoking Situation:

Goal of Exposure:

Plan:
1. Rate the predicted level of anxiety for each step, below
2. Start with the first step. Stick with it for 5 minutes, or until anxiety decreases during the exposure, whichever comes first
3. Fill out Tracking Form. Rate anxiety before, during and after
4. Continue exposing self to that one step, until the anxiety rating reduces by 50% of the original predicted rating
5. Once 50% reduction is achieved, move to the next step
6. Practice as much as you'd like, aim for at least 3-5x/week

Exposure Steps;

Step	Anxiety Rating (0-100)

Exposure Tracking Form

Directions

You can use this form to track your exposure practice. Include the dates, the time you spent on the exposure, and rate how you felt before, during, and after, using the 0-100 anxiety scale. Refer to page 62 as needed.

Date	Start Time	Stop Time	Rating Before	Rating During	Rating After	Comments

Rachel Boyer, LMHC
INSIGHTFUL SOLUTIONS THERAPY

Reboot Reflection

This page is yours to explore any thoughts, themes, or insights that stood out. You'll also find a few guiding questions to support your reflection.

Something I have been avoiding...

How has this impacted my life?

One insight or pattern I noticed...

Something I want to remember...

Rachel Boyer, LMHC
INSIGHTFUL SOLUTIONS THERAPY

Managing Emotions

Emotions are powerful messengers. They signal our needs, shape our decisions, and influence how we relate to ourselves and others. But when emotions feel overwhelming, unpredictable, or stuck, they can interfere with our ability to think clearly, act intentionally, and feel safe in our own skin.

This section is designed to help you build emotional awareness, increase your tolerance for distress, and develop practical tools for soothing and shifting emotional states.

Rachel Boyer, LMHC
INSIGHTFUL SOLUTIONS THERAPY

Distress Tolerance

What?

At some point, we all encounter physical and emotional discomfort. This pain can arise suddenly, crashing over us like an overwhelming wave, leaving us feeling as though it will never end and unsure of how to cope. In moments of stress, we may resort to unhealthy coping mechanisms because we lack the tools to manage our feelings, or they just feel so intense.

Some unhealthy responses:
- Dwelling on past hurts or worrying excessively about future pain
- Withdrawing from others or avoiding stressful circumstances
- Using substances or engaging in harmful behaviors to numb the pain
- Misusing food, exercise, or other activities as an escape
- Evading the issue or resigning ourselves to endure its misery

These unhealthy responses can have detrimental effects, leading to prolonged suffering rather than relief.

The truth is that painful moments are an inevitable part of life; they cannot be avoided or eliminated but must be tolerated. Developing distress tolerance skills can enable you to cope with pain in healthier ways, preventing it from spiraling into ongoing suffering. These skills may include distraction, self-soothing, grounding and acceptance.

Distraction

Distraction serves as a valuable skill that allows you to momentarily shift your focus away from your pain, providing you with the necessary time to discover healthier coping mechanisms. It is not intended to help you avoid stressful situations but rather to create space for your emotions to settle so that you can later approach the problem with a clear mind. There are numerous strategies for distraction.

Distraction: Techniques

Attention on Others

Shift your attention to someone else:

- Ask friends, family or neighbors if there is anything you can help with. Take someone out for lunch. Volunteer.
- Watch others. Go to a store and observe. Listen to conversations, see what they are wearing, watch what they do.
- Think of someone you care about. Look at a picture of them. Imagine them.

Helpful Thoughts

Replace unhelpful with pleasing thoughts:

- Remember past positive experiences and replay the memories in detail.
- Observe the natural world around you- flowers, trees, animals. Use your senses and appreciate where you are.
- Keep a copy of a favorite inspirational story, a prayer, a favorite song, etc., and read it to yourself.

Tasks & Chores

Take care of yourself and your environment:

- Clean your room, dishes, closet, laundry
- Donate things you get rid of.
- Take a bath or shower.
- Water your plants or tend to a garden.
- Go food shopping and cook dinner.

Count

Keep your mind busy:

- Count your breaths.
- Count what you're hearing or seeing (ex., cars passing by).
- Count or subtract by a certain number (ex., count backwards from 100 by 2).

Rachel Boyer, LMHC
INSIGHTFUL SOLUTIONS THERAPY

Soothe With Senses

Use your five senses to help de-stress and reduce the intensity of emotions.

Vision

- Look at pictures
- Watch nature or sunrise/set
- Light a candle & watch the flame
- View the stars at night
- Buy a beautiful flower
- Make your space pleasing to look at

Hearing

- Listen to music
- Pay attention to sounds in nature
- Listen to sounds in the city
- Use a guided meditation app
- Learn an instrument
- Listen to a water fountain

Smell

- Use your favorite soap or shampoo
- Try on perfume, cologne, lotions
- Light incense or candles
- Smell nature- the air, cut grass, ocean
- Walk and find flowers
- Boil cinnamon or bake cookies

Taste

- Eat your favorite food
- Drink hot chocolate, tea or a latte
- Taste cold ice cream or a smoothie
- Eat a favorite from childhood
- Suck on peppermint or chocolate
- Chew some gum

Touch

- Take a hot bath or shower
- Pet your animals
- Get a massage or pedicure
- Wear a soft sweatshirt
- Rub textures like velvet or smooth rocks
- Go for a drive with the windows down

Rachel Boyer, LMHC
INSIGHTFUL SOLUTIONS THERAPY

Sensory Awareness

Consider participating in a sensory awareness exercise. You can either record the questions listed below or choose another guided activity that suits you. Get into a comfortable position and allow yourself at least five seconds to reflect on each question.

1. Are you aware of your hair brushing against your head?
2. Can you sense your belly rising and falling as you breathe?
3. Can you feel the space between your eyes?
4. Can you perceive the distance between your ears?
5. Do you notice your breath reaching the back of your eyes as you inhale?
6. Can you visualize something far away?
7. Are you aware of your arms making contact with your body?
8. Can you feel the soles of your feet?
9. Can you envision a beautiful day at the beach?
10. Are you conscious of the space inside your mouth?
11. Can you notice the position of your tongue within your mouth?
12. Can you feel a gentle breeze against your cheek?
13. Are you aware of one arm feeling heavier than the other?
14. Can you sense any tingling or numbness in one of your hands?
15. Do you feel that one arm is more relaxed than the other?
16. Can you detect a change in the temperature of the air around you?
17. Are you aware that your left arm feels warmer than the right?
18. Can you imagine the sensation of being a rag doll?
19. Do you notice any tightness in your left forearm?
20. Can you envision something very pleasant?
21. Can you imagine the feeling of floating on a cloud?
22. Can you picture what it would be like to be stuck in molasses?
23. Can you visualize something in the distance?
24. Are you aware of a heaviness in your legs?
25. Can you imagine floating in warm water?
26. Can you sense your body hanging gently from your bones?
27. Are you able to allow yourself to drift lazily?
28. Can you feel your face becoming soft?
29. Can you envision a beautiful flower?
30. Are you aware of one arm and leg feeling heavier than the other?

Rachel Boyer, LMHC
INSIGHTFUL SOLUTIONS THERAPY

Grounding

Why?

When emotions get overwhelming, grounding can help you stay in the present moment rather than being distracted by internal thoughts and negative feelings. Practice by focusing on the physical world you are in, using all of your senses, and let go of focusing on the negative thoughts. See if any of the below work for you, or make up your own.

Splash cold water on your hands or face

Clench and release your fists

Touch objects around you

Feel a soothing object (i.e. smooth rock)

Dig your heels into the ground

Wiggle your toes

Stretch or roll your head

Focus on your breathing

Move your body: jog in place or jump

Listen to soothing music

Describe what's around you

Notice what you see, hear, and smell

Rachel Boyer, LMHC
INSIGHTFUL SOLUTIONS THERAPY

Acceptance

Radical Acceptance

Changing your attitude will increase your ability to tolerate distress. Radical acceptance is the ability to look at yourself or a situation, and seeing it for what it really is. This doesn't mean you agree with a situation, it just means that you are accepting it's out of your control and it's better to focus on what you can do now.

Radical acceptance coping statements:
- This is the way it has to be
- I can't change what has already happened
- It's no use fighting the past
- It's a waste of time fighting the past, let me focus on today
- This moment is as it is
- The facts are the facts, even if I don't like them

Why Accept Reality?

Refusing to accept reality keeps you stuck in painful emotions like unhappiness, anger, shame and sadness

Rejecting or getting upset about reality does not change it

Accepting reality may lead to sadness, but calmness usually follows

Changing your current reality requires accepting reality for what it has been

Rejecting reality turns pain into ongoing suffering

Rachel Boyer, LMHC
INSIGHTFUL SOLUTIONS THERAPY

Acceptance

Practicing Radical Acceptance

Sometimes, we face uncontrollable situations that are painful. Radical acceptance helps evaluate these circumstances and lessen emotional burdens like resentment or anger. Use the following prompts to practice radical acceptance.

What's bothering you?

What events led to this reality? Is there something here you have to accept (facts that can't be changed)?

What emotions do you feel? Sit with your emotions. It's o.k. to feel them.

Where in your body do you feel your emotions? Practice feeling and then releasing them.

Imagine how'd you change your behaviors if you accepted this reality. What would it feel like to let it go?

Imagine what it feels like to accept this reality. What can you tell yourself to help accept it?

Despite the pain of this reality, what makes life worth living? How can I move on from this?

Rachel Boyer, LMHC
INSIGHTFUL SOLUTIONS THERAPY

"STOP" Technique

Why?

Distress tolerance skills, such as the "STOP" Technique, help manage intense emotions and impulsive behaviors without harmful coping mechanisms. This mindfulness practice encourages pausing to slow down a racing mind, which benefits mental well-being, even with brief breaks.

Stop

Interrupt your thoughts with the command 'stop!' and pause whatever you're doing.

Take a Breath

Notice your breathing for a second. Breathe in gently and slowly through your nose, expanding your belly as you do, and exhale slowly through pursed lips.

Observe

Become the observer of your thoughts, emotions and physical sensations. What thoughts do you notice? What emotions are surfacing? How does your body feel? Tune in and stay with whatever arises for a few moments.

Proceed

Mindfully consider how you'd like to respond. What's one small thing you can focus on right now? What would be a helpful response to this situation? Narrow down your focus and take it one small step at a time.

Rachel Boyer, LMHC
INSIGHTFUL SOLUTIONS THERAPY

Emotion Regulation

Why?

Recognizing and processing emotions can sometimes feel overwhelming, and choosing to avoid them may result in unhealthy thoughts or behaviors. Here are a few steps you can take to respond to unhelpful emotions in a more constructive manner.

How?

When you become aware of a feeling, take a moment to PAUSE. Observe and describe the emotion; label it. Consider how it feels and where you experience it in your body. What event triggered this feeling?

Reflect on the role emotions play in your life. They can motivate us to take action, communicate with others, and convey messages to ourselves.

Understand why regulating emotions can be challenging. Factors such as our biology, lack of experience, or deeply held beliefs can influence how we respond to them.

Separate yourself from your emotions —remember, you are not defined by them. Avoid judgment and accept their presence. You don't always have to act on how you feel; think of emotions as waves that rise and fall.

Allow the emotions to drift away, like leaves floating on a stream. If you find this hard, try self-soothing or grounding techniques such as progressive muscle relaxation, taking a warm shower, focusing on your favorite things, or practicing deep breathing.

Reduce the likelihood of being overwhelmed by emotions in the future. Engage in Cognitive Behavioral Therapy (CBT), prioritize self-care, and cultivate positive emotions through new experiences.

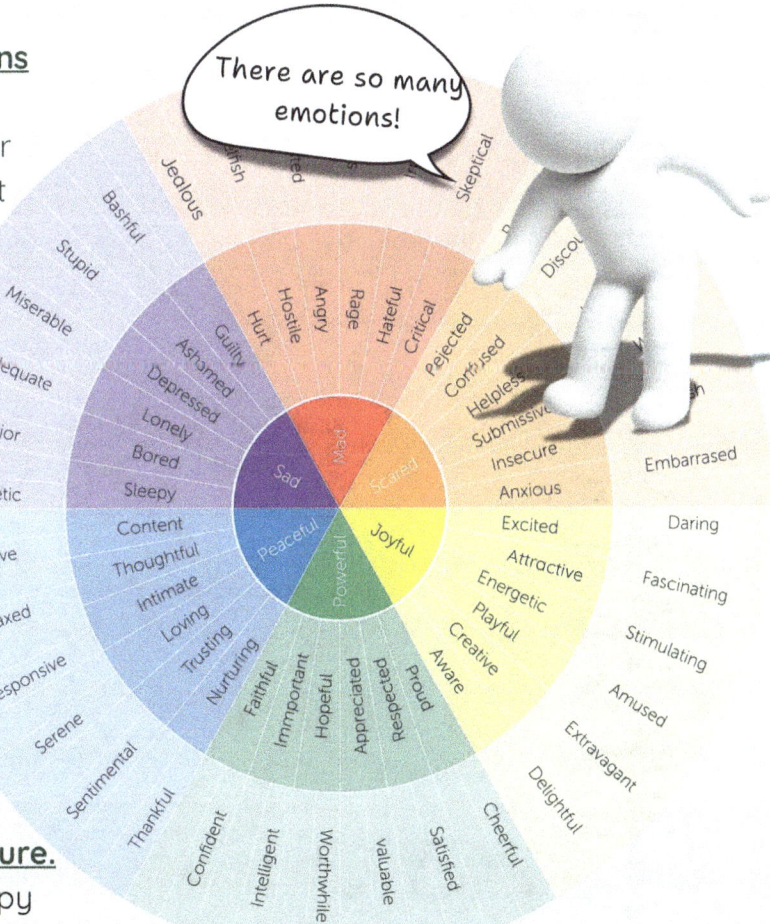

Reboot Reflection

This page is yours to explore any thoughts, themes, or insights that stood out. You'll also find a few guiding questions to support your reflection.

A new skill I want to try is...

My plan to practice this is...

One insight or pattern I noticed...

Something I want to remember...

Rachel Boyer, LMHC
INSIGHTFUL SOLUTIONS THERAPY

Practice, track, and strengthen what works.

Coping skills are more than just tools—they're lifelines that help us navigate stress, regulate emotions, and reconnect with our values when life feels overwhelming. This section offers simple, structured templates to help you track what works, notice patterns, and build a personalized toolkit of strategies that support your wellbeing.

Whether you're experimenting with grounding techniques, emotion regulation strategies, or behavioral shifts, these pages are designed to help you test and track what works.

Rachel Boyer, LMHC
INSIGHTFUL SOLUTIONS THERAPY

Coping Skills Scenario Practice

Practice preparing for stressful events or scenarios by identifying which coping tools may help you. You can use the questions below as a guide.

Coping Skills Scenario Practice

Scenario:

Which tools help with thoughts, emotions and behaviors:

- ☐
- ☐
- ☐
- ☐
- ☐

What's my first step (to prepare):

What I want to remember in the moment:

My Coping Tool Box

List your favorite coping skills to build a toolbox that will help you feel grounded and supported when you need it.

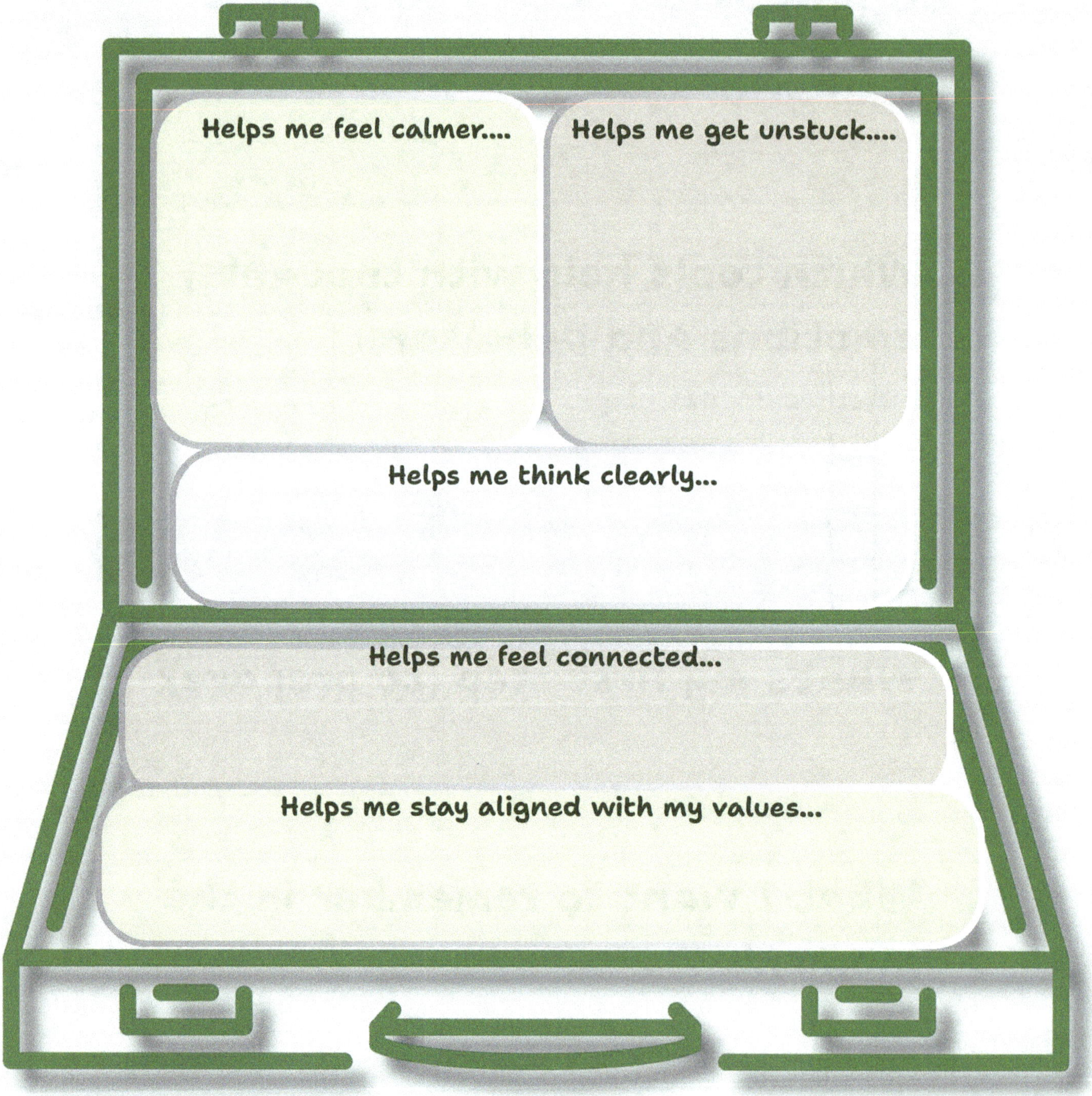

Helps me feel calmer....

Helps me get unstuck.....

Helps me think clearly...

Helps me feel connected...

Helps me stay aligned with my values...

Rachel Boyer, LMHC
INSIGHTFUL SOLUTIONS THERAPY

My Relapse Prevention Plan

Triggers....

Warning Signs...

What I can do....

- [ ]
- [ ]
- [ ]
- [ ]
- [ ]
- [ ]
- [ ]

My motivation...

Rachel Boyer, LMHC
INSIGHTFUL SOLUTIONS THERAPY

Reboot Reflection

This page is yours to explore any thoughts, themes, or insights that stood out. You'll also find a few guiding questions to support your reflection.

A place I can keep my skills visible:

One skill that has helped recently:

One insight or pattern I noticed...

Something I want to remember...

Rachel Boyer, LMHC
INSIGHTFUL SOLUTIONS THERAPY

Self-Compassion

Self-compassion is the practice of treating yourself with the same care, understanding, and support you would offer a loved one in pain. It's not about ignoring mistakes or avoiding growth—it's about creating a safe internal space where healing and change can take root.

This section invites you to explore what it means to be gentle with yourself in moments of distress, disappointment, or self-doubt.

Rachel Boyer, LMHC
INSIGHTFUL SOLUTIONS THERAPY

Self-Compassion

Self-compassion is the practice of treating yourself with the same kindness, understanding, and support that you would offer to someone you deeply care about—especially in moments of pain, failure, or self-doubt. It's not self-pity or self-indulgence; it's a courageous act of emotional honesty and care.

Instructions: Think of a recent moment when you were hard on yourself. Use this worksheet to shift your inner dialogue toward compassion.

If I spoke to myself like a Friend......

1. Describe the Situation
What happened? What triggered self-criticism?

_____
_____
_____

2. What Did You Say to Yourself?
Write down your inner thoughts or self-talk.

_____
_____
_____

3. Imagine a Friend in the Same Situation
What would you say to them?

_____
_____
_____
_____

4. Rewrite Your Inner Dialogue
Using the same kindness, rewrite what you'd say to yourself.

_____
_____
_____
_____

5. Anchor Phrase
Create a short phrase you can use next time you feel self-critical (e.g., "I'm doing the best I can").

_____
_____
_____

Self-Compassion

Continue to practice treating yourself with the same kindness, understanding, and support that you would extend to a loved one, particularly during times of pain, failure, or self-doubt. It is not about self-pity or indulgence; rather, it is a brave act of emotional honesty and care.

Instructions: Write a letter to yourself from the perspective of someone who loves you unconditionally. This could be a wise mentor, a future version of yourself, or even your inner caregiver.

Compassionate Letter to Myself

Dear [Your Name],

I see that you're going through...

_____

_____

I want you to know...

_____

_____

Even when you feel...

_____

_____

You are still...

_____

_____

I admire your...

_____

You deserve...

_____

_____

With love and compassion, [Signature or Symbol]

_____

Rachel Boyer, LMHC
INSIGHTFUL SOLUTIONS THERAPY

Letter to Future Self

This worksheet helps you write a compassionate message to yourself for a future moment when you're struggling. It's a way to reconnect with your strength, values, and the tools that support you—even when things feel hard.

Step 1: Set the Scene	Step 2: Validate the Experience
Imagine a future version of you who's feeling overwhelmed, stuck, or disconnected. You're writing to that version with care and understanding.	Acknowledge what this future version of you might be feeling. Offer empathy and remind yourself that it's okay to struggle.
Step 3: Reflect on What You've Learned	Step 4: Offer Kindness and Encouragement
Remind yourself of the tools, insights, and values you've practiced. Share what's helped you in the past.	Speak to yourself like you would to a close friend. Use a tone that's gentle, steady, and affirming.

Step 5: Reconnect with Your Values
Close your letter with a reminder of what matters most to you and how you want to show up for yourself.

_____
_____
_____
_____
_____
_____
_____
_____
_____
_____
_____
_____
_____
_____
_____
_____
_____

Reboot Reflection

This page is yours to explore any thoughts, themes, or insights that stood out. You'll also find a few guiding questions to support your reflection.

One phrase I want to keep as a reminder when struggling:

One kind thing I can do for myself this week:

One insight or pattern I noticed...

Something I want to remember...

Rachel Boyer, LMHC
INSIGHTFUL SOLUTIONS THERAPY

Closing- Relapse Prevention

You've made it to the final chapter. That's not just a milestone—it's a reflection of your effort, curiosity, and willingness to engage with change. This section is here to help you carry what you've learned forward, especially when life gets messy or momentum fades.

Relapse doesn't mean failure—it means you're human. Change is rarely linear, and setbacks are part of the process. What matters most is how you respond, reflect, and recommit to your goals when things get hard.

This final section helps you build a personalized plan to recognize early warning signs, respond to triggers, and identify skills and supports that keep you grounded. You'll also revisit the Reboot Reflection to check in with the insights you've gained, and the tools you've practiced.

Relapse Prevention Planning

It's essential to prepare for relapse by having tools ready to maintain success. Reflect on warning signs that hint at regression, identify triggers, and consider steps to prevent or lessen symptoms.

Warning Signs

Checkbox	Feelings/Thoughts	Early Warning	Comes Quick	First Recognized by Ohters
	Feeling irritable or easily overwhelmed			
	Increased anxiety or restlessness			
	Persistent sadness or emotional heaviness			
	Loss of interest or pleasure in things you usually enjoy			
	Feeling numb, disconnected, or emotionally flat			
	Increased desire to isolate or withdraw from others			
	Thoughts of death, escape, or suicide			
	Difficulty concentrating or making decisions			
	Feeling hopeless about the future			
	Harsh self-criticism or increased self-doubt			
	Feeling guilty or like a burden to others			

Checkbox	Behaviors	Early Warning	Comes Quick	First Recognized by Ohters
	Avoiding social contact or canceling plans			
	Sleeping significantly more or less than usual			
	Changes in appetite—eating too much or too little			
	Neglecting hygiene, chores, or daily responsibilities			
	Missing work, school, or important appointments			
	Using substances to cope or numb emotions			
	Engaging in risky or impulsive behaviors			
	Crying frequently or feeling unable to cry			
	Spending excessive time online or zoning out			
	Ignoring texts, emails, or calls			
	Losing interest in hobbies or creative outlets			
	Expressing hopelessness or giving away belongings			

Checkbox	Others	Early Warning	Comes Quick	First Recognized by Ohters

94

Relapse Prevention Planning

Being aware of triggers allows for better preparation and swift response, reducing relapse risk. Create a plan outlining steps to take when encountering triggers or warning signs, and store it in a convenient location for easy access.

Action Plan

Checkbox	Triggers	Examples/Comments
	High levels of stress	
	Changes in sleep patters	
	Recreational drug or alcohol use	
	Seasonal changes	
	Life changes (i.e. a move, job, divorce)	
	Loss or bereavement	
	Trauma or abuse	
	Difficult life conditions (i.e. housing, money, relationships)	
	Medication side effect	
	Physical illness	

Checkbox	Plan	Examples/Comments
	Understand triggers	
	Monitor moods	
	Learn warning signs	
	Develop a self management plan	

Checkbox	Action Steps	Examples/Comments
	Maintain sleep schedule	
	Avoid alcohol, drugs, caffeine	
	Engage in social activities	
	Get outside- expose self to sunlight	
	Engage in physical activity	
	Do relaxation or deep breathing exercises	
	Do activities you once enjoyed	
	Self-talk or affirmations	
	Maintain daily structure and routine	
	Continue taking prescribed medications	
	Maintain a healthy diet	
	Use family/friends/peers/community for support	
	Reach out to treatment team or emergency services if needed	

Reboot Reflection

This page is yours to explore any thoughts, themes, or insights that stood out. You'll also find a few guiding questions to support your reflection.

One warning sign I want to watch out for:

One strategy or support I'll use when I notice it:

My biggest insights or patterns I noticed...

Things I want to remember...

Rachel Boyer, LMHC
INSIGHTFUL SOLUTIONS THERAPY

Reboot Reset

Reflect on your initial goal, the changes you've made, and the skills you've gained. Review how you'll apply your learnings in the future, and identify areas that may need a refresh.

What was your original challenge and goal?

How have your thoughts, feelings and behaviors shifted?

How do you feel with your progress on this goal?

What skills will you continue to use going forward?

Check out the Skills Checklist on the next page!

What are your next steps after this?

Rachel Boyer, LMHC
INSIGHTFUL SOLUTIONS THERAPY

Reboot Reset

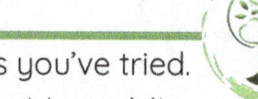

As you reflect on your activities in this workbook, check off the skills you've tried. Note which ones are most helpful, least helpful, or ones that you want to revisit.

My Skill Checklist

SKILL	Tried it?	Notes
Identifying automatic thoughts	☐	
Recognizing "HOT" thoughts	☐	
Spotting cognitive distortions	☐	
Using thought records	☐	
Cognitive restructuring	☐	
Challenging beliefs	☐	
Mood tracking	☐	
Monitoring emotional patterns over time	☐	
Identifying body-based emotional cues	☐	
Naming and rating emotions	☐	
Recognizing emotional triggers	☐	
Identifying core issues	☐	
Clarifying personal goals	☐	
Exploring core beliefs	☐	
Tracing origins of beliefs	☐	
Testing and updating beliefs	☐	
Practicing self-kindness in moments of distress	☐	
Noticing the inner critic and softening its tone	☐	
Creating affirming self-statements	☐	
Building emotional safety through reflection	☐	
Tracking coping skill use and effectiveness	☐	
Identifying go-to strategies and expanding the toolkit	☐	
Reflecting on what helps in moments of distress	☐	
Recognizing early warning signs	☐	
Identifying personal vulnerability patterns	☐	
Creating a relapse response plan	☐	

Rachel Boyer, LMHC
INSIGHTFUL SOLUTIONS THERAPY

Thank You!!

Thank you for your commitment and courage in using this workbook. Remember, the insights and tools you've gained are not just for this moment, but are for a lifetime. Thank you for trusting me to be a part of your journey.

~Rachel Boyer, LMHC
Insightful Solutions Therapy

Want More?

KEEP THE MOMENTUM GOING

You can download free resources and printable versions of the trackers in this workbook by visiting **www.InsightfulSolutionsTherapy.org** or using the QR Code below, and accessing the "Resources" section.

Use them to practice your goals, track your progress, and stay grounded in the skills you've learned.

MORE TOOLKITS ON THE WAY!

Upcoming volumes in The Mind Reboot Toolkit series will focus on important topics like anxiety, depression, and eating disorders. Each volume will offer practical strategies and insights tailored to individual needs. These resources are perfect for anyone looking to support their personal growth journey or to assist others on theirs.

For launch announcements and previews of upcoming toolkits, follow and subscribe to the Insightful Solutions Therapy website by visiting **www.InsightfulSolutionsTherapy.org** or scanning the QR Code below.

Rachel Boyer, LMHC
Insightful Solutions Therapy, LLC